STORY SECRETS FROM SCRIPTURE

Develop & Deliver Children's Stories for Worship, VBS & Bible Study

DOUGLAS G. PRATT

NotesForLearning.com

©2019 Douglas G. Pratt
Instagram: 88notes2happiness
Web: NotesForLearning.com/secrets
Contact: StorySecretsBook@gmail.com

Story Secrets from Scripture: Develop and Deliver Children's Stories for Worship, VBS and Bible Study

ISBN
978-0-9791486-2-0 Paperback
979-8-4831620-6-3 Hardcover

Bible versions used include the *New King James Version*, *World English Bible*, and *New International Version*. Many of the parables have been rewritten by Douglas Pratt.

INTRODUCTION

The phrase "It came to pass" is used 176 times in the *New King James Version* of the Bible. Each time, this is a cue that some action is about to occur. For a story to be a story, activity is essential—something must happen! I wrote this short book to help storytellers prepare and deliver children's stories with a focus on the action. As you will see, the Bible contains a formula for telling stories that is action-oriented. This secret is about to be revealed!

The abilities of storytellers span a continuum from those who have never told a story or even shared in public to those who are seasoned professionals in public speaking and ministry. Some individuals seem naturally gifted with the intuitive ability to tell a story without any preparation. Others require as much time as possible to prepare.

Regardless of where you are on the storytelling continuum, you will find insights in this book. If you are an experienced storyteller, restudying the parables of Jesus and mindfulness about structure will improve how you tell stories. If you have never told a story, you can use the lessons from Jesus and the framework presented here to develop and deliver stories in multiple settings. If you simply enjoy learning about the parables or learning about the craft of storytelling, you will appreciate this perspective of Bible-based storytelling.

I hope you will enjoy *Story Secrets from Scripture*.

Contents

CHAPTER 1 - SETTING THE STAGE 7
- Potential challenges to the effectiveness of a children's story.
- The importance of structure in various aspects of life.
- The analysis of stories (a brief introduction).

CHAPTER 2 - A BIBLE-BASED STRUCTURE 19
- A five-part, Bible-based structure to use when telling stories.
- Examples from the Bible to illustrate the five-part structure.

CHAPTER 3 - PARABLES OF JESUS 27
- Examples from the parables of Jesus to illustrate the five-part structure.

CHAPTER 4 - HOW JESUS SHARED PARABLES 43
- Ways to introduce and conclude a story using the techniques of Jesus.
- The variety of themes of Jesus' parables.

CHAPTER 5 - FINDING STORIES 59
- How to find stories from your own experiences.
- Guidelines for choosing stories.
- Stories from my life (including my family) illustrating the five-part structure.

CHAPTER 6 - ORIENTED TIMES THREE 77
- Ways to orient your audience to the story.
- How to use different points-of-view.
- Considerations for telling stories from different perspectives.

CHAPTER 7 - PREPARING FOR STORYTIME 91
- Seven practical techniques to ensure effective delivery of a children's story.

CHAPTER 8 AFTER THE STORY 105
- Packing up after a story.
- Ways to obtain feedback.
- How to plan for more storytelling.

THEMES IN THE BIBLE 110

1.

SETTING THE STAGE

> In this chapter you will learn about:
> - Potential challenges to the effectiveness of a children's story.
> - The importance of structure in various aspects of life.
> - The analysis of stories (a brief introduction).

My church has designated a special part of the worship service for children. As a church pianist I have a front-row seat for this children's story time. Each week, as the children leave their parents and come to the front of the sanctuary, pianists play softly. Once the children are settled and the storyteller has come to the front, the music ends, and the children's story time begins.

From my close-up perspective, I have an opportunity to see how the children react to the story and the teller. Do they pay careful attention to a compelling story or do they quickly lose focus for the duration of the story? Does an actual story or just a spiritual thought intended for adults occur? I have seen successful use of the children's story time as well as times where opportunities to share a memorable story were missed.

Missed Opportunities

In thinking about why some children's stories are more impactful than others, contributing factors fall in three key areas. The storytelling triangle visually displays the critical elements necessary for a successful children's story: the storyteller, the children (audience), and the story itself. All three elements are essential. If any component or combination is not optimized, the story experience will not be as impactful.

This graphic illustrates the interactions of the storyteller, the story, and the audience. Each has a role in the story experience.

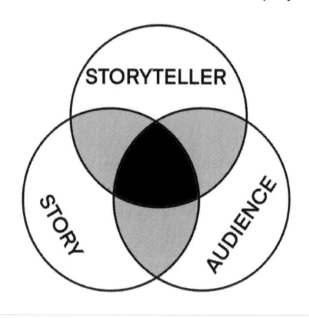

Storyteller

Some individuals naturally excel at telling a story, a few clearly cannot, and the rest fall somewhere in between. Storytellers must

SETTING THE STAGE

be physically ready and emotionally present to effectively tell a story. If storytellers have not thought about their stories in advance, this lack of preparation is often revealed as the "story" progresses. What's key is that each of us—regardless of the role in a service or program—must be willing to improve the talents God has given us.

> Be diligent to present yourself approved to God (2 Timothy 2:15).

> By diligent effort all may acquire the power to read intelligently, and to speak in a full, clear, round tone, in a distinct and impressive manner. (Ellen G. White, *Christ's Object Lessons*, p335).

Children

An element largely out of the control of the storyteller is the audience. The range of ages and personalities of children present challenges for even seasoned storytellers. I recently attended a church where one toddler interrupted nearly every sentence to ask a question or introduce his own thoughts as the story unfolded. Children's physical and cognitive abilities continue to develop during the ages when children usually participate as part of a children's story audience. Children often have limited attention spans, even with the most dynamic storytellers.

Between the ages of 5-7 children begin developing reasoning skills. Until then children understand stories literally because that's all they know. Abstract concepts like love, character, and revelation must be communicated to children in simple and plain language they understand in the same way Jesus did—with stories and object lessons.

STORY SECRETS FROM SCRIPTURE

Jean Piaget was an early childhood researcher in the early twentieth century. He created an experiment where he showed two balls of clay to a young child. After the child agreed they were the same size, Piaget reformed one ball into a cylinder shape while the child watched. He then asked the child which one had more clay, the ball or the cylinder. Answers varied. As their brains develop, Piaget theorized, children begin to think logically about concrete things. Children in this stage of development understood that the volume of clay was unchanged regardless of shape. But children who had not yet developed these skills responded that either the ball or the cylinder had a larger volume of clay. I repeated this experiment with first graders as part of a developmental psychology course. My results were like Piaget's.

Story

The story told by the storyteller to the children contributes to the success of a children's story experience. Sometimes "stories" are not really stories. Recently I heard a children's story where the storyteller mentioned random Bible characters, but never told stories about any of them. Other times a story can include unnecessary details that only result in lengthening the story. Some stories can have complicated plots that may be confusing to an audience of children. Complicated plots require more time to unfold and to conclude.

For example, the story of Jacob in the Bible spans 147 years (and 25 chapters of Genesis). It includes the stories of Judah and Tamar, Esau, and Joseph within the main narrative of Jacob. This entire narrative cannot be told in three to five minutes, the length of a typical children's story. Additionally, the story of Judah and Tamar (Genesis 38:1-26) centers around a complicated sexual encounter, a topic inappropriate for a children's story.

In their book, *Made to Stick: Why Some Ideas Survive and Others Die* (2008), brothers Chip and Dan Heath presented a theory on why some ideas are memorable, but others are not. For example, you may quickly be able to recall the details of an urban legend (such as a story about someone drugged then having a kidney stolen or getting shot if you flash your lights at an oncoming car with its lights off) but you may have difficulty recalling the sermon from two weeks ago.

The authors defined six variables to help ideas become *stickier*. These variables were arranged to form the acronym SUCCESS. Keep ideas *Simple* by focusing on the core message. Reveal something *Unexpected* to differentiate your message from others. Present your idea or message in a *Concrete*, tangible way so the recipients or audience are more likely to quickly grasp it. Establish *Credibility* by inviting your audience to apply an idea or try a product—test it out for themselves. Create an *Emotional* connection by crafting a message that resonates at a deeper level. Finally, use *StorieS* so that others can easily recall and share your message.

A slight modification of the acronym in *Made to Stick*—and a reordering—fits perfectly to define what a successful children's story looks like.

Simple and Concrete - Stories need to align with the cognitive needs of children - concrete thinking, simple language, and limited attention spans.

Unexpected and Emotional - Elements of surprise where children are drawn into the story results in a more memorable story.

Concise and Structured - Children's stories need to fit within a shorter period, and following a structure helps effectively tell a story in the time allotted.

Importance of Structure

The *Oxford American Dictionary* (3RD edition) defines *structure* as:

NOUN The arrangement of and relations between the parts of something complete.

VERB Organize or arrange something according to a plan or system.

Whether classic or modern, songs have a structure, as just defined. Sonatas have been composed for hundreds of years, but always follow a structure of exposition—the initial presentation of the melody, development—contrast to the exposition, and recapitulation—the result of harmonic dissonance and a return to the initial theme of the sonata. If a song follows this structure, it can be considered a sonata. If these structural elements do not exist, it is not a sonata. Modern songs are often structured in this way: Introduction, Verse 1, Chorus, Verse 2, Chorus, Bridge, Chorus (often repeated multiple times), Ending. Even though an underlying structure exists, millions of songs have been written, and each is unique.

Structure is also evident in the layout of houses. Most modern houses have a floor plan consisting of multiple rooms. Most houses, large or small, include a front door that opens into an entryway, living room or open space. A cluster of public rooms and a series of bedrooms are arranged in different parts of the house. Have you ever seen a multi-room house where the first room you enter through the front, main door is the master bedroom? Probably not. It doesn't fit with the expected layout and is awkward. Bedrooms come with an expectation of privacy and therefore are not the first rooms visitors enter. A subdivision might be comprised of several streets of houses. Though each is different, most have the same basic conceptual structure of public rooms, bedrooms, and a kitchen.

The Beginning of Story Analysis

Successful stories also have structure. The earliest recorded definition of plot was written by Aristotle, a Greek philosopher, in his book *Poetics* (335 BC):

> A whole is that which has a beginning, a middle, and an end. A beginning is that which does not itself follow anything by causal necessity, but after which something naturally is or comes to be. An end, on the contrary, is that which itself naturally follows some other thing, either by necessity, or as a rule, but has nothing following it. A middle is that which follows something as some other thing follows it. A well-constructed plot, therefore, must

neither begin nor end at random, but conform to these principles.

According to Aristotle, a story must have a beginning, a middle, and an end. This structure can be seen in many stories, both Biblical and non-Biblical. The Bible includes a few verses that provide direct evidence of an awareness of structure by the inspired authors. Aristotle did not invent story structure. These Bible stories show us that the concept of narrative structure has existed for thousands of years.

Adam & Eve

Moses wrote the book of Genesis, one of the oldest books of the Bible. After Adam and Eve ate of the forbidden fruit (Genesis 3:6, 7), God came to the garden. "Where are you?" He asked. Once Adam and Eve came out of their hiding place, Adam gave his version of what had just occurred (Genesis 3:12):

- **Beginning** - The woman You created for me
- **Middle** - Gave me fruit from the tree.
- **End** - And I ate it.

Simply eating fruit from a tree is uninteresting. God told Adam, "You may freely eat of every tree in the garden" (Genesis 2:16), but then continued, "But you shall not eat of the tree of the knowledge of good and evil" (Genesis 2:17). Because he ate of a forbidden tree, Adam's story became interesting. God already knew what had occurred, but questioned Adam. If Adam had eaten from any other tree, he would not have realized his naked condition (Genesis 3:7).

SETTING THE STAGE

Achan

The book of Joshua includes the story of Achan. Achan disobeyed God's command not to take any valuables from the destroyed city of Jericho. Once Achan was identified as the offender, Joshua said to him, "Tell me what you have done." Achan confessed in story form (Joshua 7:21):

- **Beginning** - I saw something.
- **Middle** - I wanted it,
- **End** - So I took it.

Immediately before the walls of Jericho fell, Joshua told the army of Israel, "Be careful that you don't covet anything in the city because everything is cursed. However, all the gold, silver, bronze, and iron are holy to the Lord. Put them in God's treasury" (Joshua 6:18, 19). Achan's actions were in direct opposition to the command of Joshua, God's messenger and leader of the children of Israel. It was because of the conflict between the command of Joshua and the actions of Achan that this story was included in the book of Joshua. If Achan had complied with the command, nothing unexpected would have occurred.

Gideon

In Judges, Gideon was directed by God to lead Israel against the Midianites (Judges 6:11-8:32). Gideon was a hesitant leader and frequently sought confirmation from God. At one point, Gideon slipped into the camp of the Midianites at night where he heard one soldier say to another, "I have had a dream. A loaf of barley bread tumbled into the camp of Midian. It struck a tent, and the tent collapsed." This short narrative (Judges 7:13) is a

story that fits the structure described by Aristotle but written a millennium before.
- **Beginning** - A tent was standing (implied)
- **Middle** - A loaf of bread hit the tent.
- **End** - The tent collapsed.

A tent is designed to stand once erected. In the dream, something expected—a standing tent—met an untimely end because of unexpected intruder, the loaf of bread.

Luke

The physician Luke, author of Luke and Acts, introduced his gospel with the statement: "It seemed good to me also, having had perfect understanding of all things from the very first, to write to you an orderly account" (Luke 1:3). Starting at the beginning and following an orderly structure is not only effective, it is Biblical.

In Acts 10, a Gentile named Cornelius was instructed by an angel to send men to Joppa, where Peter was staying. While the men were traveling towards him, Peter received a vision that the Gospel message should go to the Gentiles. When the men arrived, Peter accompanied them back to the house of Cornelius, where the Gospel was shared. Peter returned to Jerusalem and was accused by a few church leaders of acting inappropriately. Peter and others shared their experiences, paving the way to share the Gospel beyond the Jewish world. The key verse indicating a story structure is Acts 11:4, "But Peter explained it to them in order from the beginning."

SETTING THE STAGE

Demon-Possessed Man

The Gospel writers recorded the sequence of events when Jesus encountered a man possessed by demons. Jesus commanded the demons to leave the man and enter a nearby herd of pigs. The owners of the pigs asked Jesus to leave the area, which He did. The man, now freed of demons, asked Jesus to accompany Him. However, Jesus responded, "Go home to your friends and tell them what great things the Lord has done for you. Tell them how He had compassion on you" (Mark 5:19). The instruction of Jesus to "tell great things" implies a story structure. I imagine that the story told by the man could have looked like this:

- **Beginning** - I was possessed by demons when Jesus found me.
- **Middle** - The demons talked to Jesus through me, but Jesus sent them into a herd of pigs.
- **End** - Now I am free from demons because Jesus had compassion on me.

Summary

In this chapter you learned about setting the stage for telling stories:
1. Remember that an effective storytelling experience involves a storyteller who seeks to continually improve, an audience whose characteristics are known, and a story that is right-sized for the time allotted and appropriate for children.
2. Keep in mind that successful stories are often simple, concrete, unexpected, emotional, concise, and structured.
3. Apply structure to ensure that a story is cohesive and flows well.
4. Recall that one timeless structure is beginning, middle, end.

2.

BIBLE-BASED STRUCTURE

> In this chapter you will learn about:
> - A five-part, Bible-based structure to use when telling stories.
> - Examples from the Bible to illustrate the five-part structure.

Many books and articles about story structure have been published. The number of elements contained in various structures range from three, based on Aristotle, to forty! In between are books that advocate four parts, eight parts, and twelve parts. Instead of including all these different structures, I selected one structure ideally suited to short, parable-style storytelling.

The Five-Part Structure

The structure I am introducing here—and will be used throughout this book—has five parts. Five seems to be a good number because it is easy to remember but provides a little more detail than a simple beginning, middle, and end. A three- to five-minute story does not require the same complexity as a full-length book or a movie.

INITIAL SITUATION
In the initial situation, the main character is living a routine, normal life. Nothing out of the ordinary has occurred. Details relevant to the setup of the story are told.

COMPLICATIONS
Something happens to interrupt the ordinary, every-day world of the main character. More than one complication may occur.

ACTION
The main character responds to the complication(s) by taking one or more actions.

RESULT
These actions have outcomes, either successful or unsuccessful.

FINAL SITUATION
After any cycles of complications-actions-results have concluded, the story ends with the final situation. After everything in the story has occurred, how did it end? The French word *denouement* means *tying up*, and this is what should occur in the Final Situation.

Examples

These stories from the Bible illustrate the five-part structure.

BIBLE-BASED STRUCTURE

Peter's Mother-in-Law Healed
MATTHEW 8:14, 15

When Jesus enter Peter's house, He saw his wife's mother lying sick with a fever. He touched her hand, and the fever left her. She arose and served them.

These two short verses provide a clear example of the five-part story structure.

INITIAL SITUATION
Jesus entered Peter's house.

COMPLICATIONS
Peter's mother-in-law was sick with a fever.

ACTION
Jesus touched her hand.

RESULT
The fever left her.

FINAL SITUATION
She got up and served them.

STORY SECRETS FROM SCRIPTURE

Lost Sheep

LUKE 15:4-6

> If a man had 100 sheep, but lost one of them, he would leave the 99 and go searching everywhere for the one lost sheep. Once he found it, he would carry it home on his shoulders and place it back in the pen with the other sheep. Then, that man would call his friends and say, "Rejoice with me, for I have found my sheep that was lost!"

INITIAL SITUATION
A man had 100 sheep.

COMPLICATIONS
He lost one of the sheep.

ACTION
He searched for the sheep until he found it.

RESULT
He carried the sheep home and placed it with the 99 sheep.

FINAL SITUATION
He celebrated with his friends.

This parable clearly shows the structure of the story as outlined above. This story is exciting because of how the story unfolds with the complication and action. If the shepherd wrote off the lost sheep as a one-percent loss, the story would fall apart as an illustration of salvation. Likewise, if the shepherd only searched half-heartedly or gave up, the meaning would remain with the one sheep—lost! If a man had 100 sheep and nothing ever happened, this parable would not be interesting, nor would it show the story of salvation.

BIBLE-BASED STRUCTURE

Noah and the Flood

GENESIS 6-8

Not so many years after the Creation and the Fall—when God promised salvation to Adam and Eve—humans populated the earth. However, except for a few true followers of God, everyone else had become wicked. God told Noah, "In 120 years I will destroy the earth by a worldwide flood." Noah warned the people about the flood while building a large ark following a design provided by God.

When the ark was finished, at the end of the 120 years, God sent animals to the ark so that they would be preserved after the flood. After Noah entered the ark an angel shut the door. Seven days later great floods came upon the earth, the result of rain from above and springs of water from deep inside the earth. After many days of rain and many more days of the ark floating above the earth, the waters eventually subsided.

Noah and his family left the ark, followed by the animals. Noah immediately offered a sacrifice to God. God was pleased and told Noah, "Look in the sky. I have placed a rainbow there as a promise that I will never again destroy the earth by a flood."

The Flood is a more complicated story than the first two examples, but it still fits the five-part structure. The structure should not be viewed as a hard-and-fast rule that can never be broken, but as a guide to help formulate your story in a way to structure a story with a clear beginning (initial situation), middle (complications, action and result), and ending (final situation).

STORY SECRETS FROM SCRIPTURE

This table displays how the simple structure of beginning, middle, end fit with the five-part structure.

Beginning	Middle			End
Initial Situation	Complications	Action	Result	Final Situation

INITIAL SITUATION
After the Fall, the population increased.

COMPLICATIONS
Most of the population was wicked, with only a remnant left as true followers of God.

ACTION
God proclaimed that He would destroy the world with a flood but told Noah to build an ark of safety.

RESULT
A great flood came upon the earth and destroyed everything, but Noah was preserved by God in the ark.

FINAL SITUATION
Noah's faithfulness to God preserved humanity so that the promise of salvation could continue.

BIBLE-BASED STRUCTURE

Demon Possessed Man

MARK 5:1-20

Jesus and His disciples came to the country on the opposite side of Lake Galilee. Immediately as Jesus got out of the boat a demon-possessed man came to meet Him. The man had shackles on his arms and legs, but the power of the demons was so great that the chains were unable to hold the man. When the man saw Jesus, he said, "What do you want from me, Jesus, Son of the Most High God? Do not send me away."

Jesus said, "Come out of the man," and then Jesus asked, "What is your name?"

The demon replied, speaking through the man, "Legion, for we are many. Please do not send us away." Nearby, on a hill, was a herd of pigs. "Please send us into the pigs." Jesus gave them permission to enter the pigs. The herd of pigs, about 2,000, rushed down the steep bank into the lake and were drowned. The owners of the pigs came to assess the situation. They, along with most of the town's citizens asked Jesus to leave.

The man who had been demon possessed, now in his right mind, asked Jesus if he could go with Him back to the other side of the lake. But Jesus said, "No. You need to stay here and tell others about the great things the Lord has done for you. Tell them how the Lord had mercy on you."

STORY SECRETS FROM SCRIPTURE

The man went throughout the countryside telling how much Jesus had done for him, and the people were amazed.

INITIAL SITUATION
A demon possessed man met Jesus at the shore. Jesus commanded the demons to leave the man.

COMPLICATIONS
The demon begged not to be sent away, but instead into a herd of pigs.

ACTION
Jesus consented, the demon entered the pigs and the pigs rushed down the hill and drowned in the lake.

RESULT
The owner of the pigs and the entire town asked Jesus to leave.

FINAL SITUATION
The previously demon possessed man stayed behind and told everyone what Jesus had done for him.

Summary

In this chapter your learned about a Bible-based structure for telling stories:
1. Start with the *initial situation*.
2. Add one or more *complications* to make the story interesting.
3. Share the *actions* characters take to resolve complications.
4. Provide the *result* of the actions.
5. End with the *final situation*.

3.
PARABLES OF JESUS

In this chapter you will learn about:
- Examples from the parables of Jesus to illustrate the five-part structure.

Jesus told many parables. Counts vary by whether versions of parables in different books are combined and whether object lessons are included. The parables included in this section represent a small sample I selected to illustrate the five-part structure.

STORY SECRETS FROM SCRIPTURE

The Wheat and the Tares
MATTHEW 13:24-30

> The kingdom of heaven is like a man who sowed good seed in his field. But while people slept, his enemy came and sowed tares among the wheat and went his way. When the grain sprouted and produced a crop, the tares also appeared.
>
> The servants of the owner came to him and asked, "Didn't you sow wheat? How then are tares growing?"
>
> The owner answered, "An enemy has done this."
>
> The servants said, "Should we pull up the tares?"
>
> The owner replied, "No, let both grow together until the harvest so that you don't uproot the wheat. Then, at the harvest, the reapers can gather the tares into bundles and burn them, but they can gather the wheat into my barn."

INITIAL SITUATION
A man sowed good seed in his field.

COMPLICATIONS
At night his enemy planted tares among the grain. As both the wheat and the tares grew, it became apparent that something was not right.

ACTION
The workers discussed the situation with the owner.

RESULT
The owner told the workers to separate the crops at the harvest.

FINAL SITUATION
The wheat was stored in the barn, but the tares were burned.

Prodigal Son

LUKE 15:11-32

A man had two sons. One day the younger came to his father and said, "Father, give me the share of the estate that belongs to me."

The father divided his assets between his sons. Not long after, the youngest son gathered all his belongings and portion of the estate and journeyed to a distant country. He squandered his share of his father's money in wild living. After he had spent everything, a famine came to that region. He soon realized that he needed shelter and food, so he found a pig farmer and agreed to work for him. He was so hungry that he even considered eating the slop given to the pigs.

After a time, he came to his senses and said, "All of my father's servants have plenty of bread to eat, but here I am perishing! I will return to my father and say, 'Father, I have sinned. I am no longer worthy to be called your son. Make me like one of your servants.'"

The son returned home, and while he was still some distance from the house, the father saw him and ran to him. The father embraced his son and cried. The son told his father what he had rehearsed, but the father said, "Bring out the best robe and put a ring on his hand. Let's celebrate, because my son was dead and is now alive again!"

STORY SECRETS FROM SCRIPTURE

While the party was going on, the older son, who had been working in the fields, asked a servant, "Why is there a party going on at the house?"

The servant replied, "Your brother has returned home!" But the older son refused to celebrate the return of his brother.

The father pleaded with him to come in to the party, but the older son said, "Look, all these years I have served you faithfully, and you never gave me an opportunity to celebrate anything with my friends."

The father replied, "Son, everything here is yours. It is right that we should celebrate and be happy. We thought your brother was gone forever, but he has returned alive and well!"

INITIAL SITUATION
A man had two sons.

COMPLICATIONS
The younger son asked for his share of the money and immediately left home. He wasted the money and resorted to feeding pigs.

ACTION
He returned home with the intention of becoming a servant to his father.

RESULT
But the father was waiting for his return and restored him as a son, complete with a celebration to welcome him home.

FINAL SITUATION
Everyone celebrated except the older brother, who felt like he had been cheated, even though the entire estate really belonged to him.

PARABLES OF JESUS

The Sower

LUKE 8:5-8 WEB

> A farmer went out to sow his seed. As he sowed, some fell along the road, and it was trampled underfoot, and the birds of the sky devoured it. Other seed fell on the rock, and as soon as it grew, it withered away because it had no moisture. Other fell amidst the thorns, and the thorns grew with it and choked it. Other seed fell into the good ground, and grew, and produced up to 100 times as much fruit.

Following a five-part structure does not mean a story must only have five singular plot points without any variation. As mentioned before, this structure is meant to serve as a guide. Seed falls into less than desirable ground three times (complications) and onto good ground one time. The multiple complications accomplish one element of the five-part structure.

INITIAL SITUATION
A farmer went out to sow his seed.

COMPLICATIONS
Some seed fell into areas where it did not mature or yield fruit.

ACTION
Some seed fell onto good ground.

RESULT
The seed grew successfully.

FINAL SITUATION
A bountiful harvest was reaped.

STORY SECRETS FROM SCRIPTURE

Wise and Foolish Builders
MATTHEW 7:24-27 NKJV

> Everyone who hears My words and does them is like a wise man who built his house on the rock. The rains descended, the floods came, and the winds blew and beat on that house, but it did not fall, for it was founded on the rock. But everyone who hears these sayings of Mine and does not do them, he will be like a foolish man who built his house on the sand. The rains descended, the floods came, and the winds blew and beat on that house, and it fell. Great was its fall.

INITIAL SITUATION
A man built his house on a rock.

COMPLICATIONS
But another man built his house on sand.

ACTION
Rains descended on both houses, floods came, and winds beat against the houses.

RESULT
The house on the rock stood firm, but the house on the rock fell flat.

FINAL SITUATION
One house survived, and one did not.

In this parable is a contrast between those who obey the words of Jesus and those who don't. This comparison still fits into a story structure. Adding the contrast of the second house is the complication ... "This way, but then that way." Naturally, different complications and actions result in different outcomes.

The Unforgiving Servant
MATTHEW 18:23-34

A king demanded that all his servants repay him for any monies they had borrowed. He called one servant to him who owed 10,000 talents. As the servant did not have the money, the king commanded that the servant and his wife and children be sold to pay down the debt.

But the servant fell down before the king and said, "Master, have patience with me, and I will repay you everything." The king was moved with compassion, released the servant's family and completely forgave the debt.

A little while later, that servant went to another servant and said, "Look, you owe me 100 denarii. Pay what you owe!"

His fellow servant fell at his feet, "Have patience with me, and I will pay my debt to you."

The first servant refused to have mercy and had the other servant put in debtor's prison. The other servants witnessed what had occurred and reported these events to the king.

The king called the servant to him again and said, "You wicked servant! I completely forgave your massive debt, but you have not had compassion on someone who

STORY SECRETS FROM SCRIPTURE

owed you a very small debt." The king put the servant in debtor's prison until all could be repaid.

INITIAL SITUATION
A king completely forgave a debt of $3,480,000,000 owed to him by a servant.

COMPLICATIONS
This same servant demanded that another servant repay him $5,800.

ACTION
When the second servant couldn't pay the debt, the first servant threw him into prison.

RESULT
The king learned what happened between his servants and informed the servant with the massive debt that he should have been compassionate towards the servant who owed the small debt.

FINAL SITUATION
The king withdrew his offer of forgiveness and placed the servant into prison until the debt could be repaid.

Both a talent and a denarius were units of currency in the New Testament times. A denarius weighed approximately four grams. A talent weighed about 33kg, equivalent to 6,000 denarii. A denarius represented a day's wages (Matthew 20:2). To understand the amounts of money in this parable, it might be helpful to convert these amounts into modern equivalents. The U.S. government has established $7.25 as a minimum wage. At this rate, a day's wage would be $58.00 ($7.25 x 8 hours). So, $58.00 x 6,000 (1 talent = 6,000 denarii) x 10,000 (number of talents owed) results in a massive debt of $3,480,000,000 ($3.5 billion)! A debt of 100 denarii would be approximately $5,800

($58.00 x 100). I used these modern equivalents in the analysis below.

Various scholars have theorized different ratios between talents and denarii. The point of this parable is that the amount owed by the first servant was so unfathomably great that he could never hope to repay it.

	$ 7.25	A
x	8.00	B
	$ 5,800.00	
x	6,000.00	C
	$ 348,000.00	
x	10,000.00	D
	$ 3,480,000,000.00	

A = U.S. minimum wage
B = Hours of work/day
C = Denarii in 1 talent
D = Number of talents in parable

STORY SECRETS FROM SCRIPTURE

Talents

MATTHEW 25:14-28

A man traveling to a far country called his servants to him. The first servant received five talents. The second servant received two talents, and the third received one talent. Immediately the man left on his journey. The first servant traded in the marketplace and earned another five talents. Likewise, the second servant traded his two talents and earned two more. But the third servant took the one talent and buried it in a hole.

After a long time, the man returned and called his servants to him. The first said, "My lord, I have doubled the talents. Here are ten talents."

The man said, "Wonderful! You have been faithful with a few things, so now I will make you ruler over many things."

The second servant gave a similar report, "I doubled your talents. Here is a total of four talents." The man congratulated the second servant and promoted him to rule over many things.

Then the third servant came and said, "My lord, you are a hard man, reaping where you have not sown, and gathering where you have not scattered. I was afraid and hid your talent in the ground. Look, here is the one talent that you gave me.

The man replied, "You are a wicked and lazy servant. Why didn't you at least deposit the talent in the bank so that would have earned interest? I am taking the talent and giving it to your fellow servant who returned ten talents to me."

INITIAL SITUATION
Before leaving on a long journey, a man gave different amounts of money to three servants:
- 5 talents ($1.75 million)
- 2 talents ($700,000)
- 1 talent ($350,000)

The servants with five and two talents made wise investments and doubled the money.

COMPLICATIONS
But the third servant buried his one talent in a hole.

ACTION
When the man returned, he demanded an accounting of the money.

RESULT
The owner praised the successful servants but condemned the third servant who had failed to deliver.

FINAL SITUATION
The successful servants were given responsibilities over large investments, but the third servant's talent was taken from him.

As with the previous parable, large amounts of money are in play. The unexpected complication is the burying of money in a hole. The rest of the story hinges on this critical complication.

STORY SECRETS FROM SCRIPTURE

Ten Virgins

MATTHEW 25:1-12

The kingdom of heaven is like ten virgins who took their lamps and went out to meet the bridegroom. Five of the virgins were wise and took extra oil with them to keep their lamps burning—just in case. However, the other five virgins were foolish and did not take any extra oil. The bridegroom was delayed, and all the virgins became drowsy and fell asleep.

At midnight a cry was heard: "Behold, the bridegroom is coming! Go out to meet him." All the virgins got up and trimmed their lamps.

The foolish said to the wise, "Give us some of your oil because our lamps our going out."

But the wise virgins replied, "No, because there will not be enough for us and for you. Go into town and buy oil for your lamps. While the foolish virgins went to buy oil, the bridegroom came, and the wedding party, including the five wise virgins, went into the wedding celebration. The door was shut.

Later, the other virgins came to the house and said, "Open the door! We are here!" But the bridegroom answered, "I don't know who you are."

PARABLES OF JESUS

INITIAL SITUATION
To help celebrate a wedding, ten virgins brought their lamps to light the way. Five brought extra oil along, but the other five did not.

COMPLICATIONS
The bridegroom was delayed.

ACTION
All the virgins fell asleep. When the bridegroom eventually passed by, the five who had brought extra oil went with the bridal party, but the others had to go buy oil. They returned and knocked on the door.

RESULT
But the door was shut.

FINAL SITUATION
The bridegroom told them that he did not know who they were and sent them away.

If the bridegroom had not been delayed the extra oil would not have been a factor because additional oil to keep the lamps burning would have been unnecessary. The delay is the complication, interrupting the expected sequence of events.

The Good Samaritan

LUKE 10:30-35

A man traveled from Jerusalem to Jericho. On the way he was attacked by thieves who stripped him of his clothing, beat him, and left him half-dead. A little while later a priest walked by on the road. When he saw the wounded man, the priest crossed to the other side of the road and passed by. A few minutes later, a Levite also walked by. He saw the wounded man and walked over

STORY SECRETS FROM SCRIPTURE

to look, but he also continued on his way. After a time, a Samaritan

riding a donkey came by. He immediately stopped, bandaged the man's wounds, set him on his donkey, and brought him to an inn, where he continued to take care of him. The next day, the Samaritan departed to continue his journey, but he gave money to the innkeeper and said, "Take care of this man. If you spend more, I will repay you on my return trip."

INITIAL SITUATION
A man traveled from Jerusalem to Jericho.

COMPLICATIONS
Thieves attacked him, stole his money and left him to die. A priest and a Levite both passed by but did not help the man.

ACTION
A Samaritan traveled the same road but stopped when he saw the injured man.

RESULT
He provided medical assistance and transported the man to a local inn.

FINAL SITUATION
The Samaritan left the man in the care of the innkeeper and promised to reimburse the innkeeper for any additional expenses.

The complications in this parable become progressively worse.

- **Complication #1** The man is robbed, stripped, and left to die.
- **Complication #2** The priest could offer help, but completely ignores the man.

- **Complication #3** The Levite passes by and looks at the man, perhaps offering the hope of help, but he does not offer any assistance.

Summary

In this chapter you learned about the parables of Jesus:
1. Use the five-part structure to plan any story.
2. Recall that the five-part structure allows for variation including multiple or progressive complications as well as numerous actions.

STORY SECRETS FROM SCRIPTURE

4.

HOW JESUS SHARED PARABLES

> In this chapter you will learn about:
> - Ways to introduce and conclude a story using the techniques of Jesus.
> - The variety of themes of Jesus' parables.

The list of parables in Chapter 3 only includes the text of the stories and a breakdown of the structure. However, Jesus did not just jump into a parable without situational context or specifically introducing and transitioning out of the parables. In this section, I will present examples from the ways Jesus approached parables and will review the different topics Jesus covered in His parables.

Introducing a Story

Introducing a story is as critical as introducing yourself to someone. Introducing a story can help set the expectations between you (the storyteller) and the audience (children).

Share the Moral First

Many children's stories are learning stories. They can be cautionary stories—outcomes to avoid—or positive stories—outcomes and behaviors to emulate. Most children's stories I have heard have an immediate transition to the moral of the story. In the world of video editing, a hard transition occurs when one scene ends abruptly and the other begins. A gentle transition occurs when one scene crossfades into the next scene. Hard transitions should be avoided in children's stories because gentle transitions allow for a smoother flow.

Jesus introduced some parables by stating the meaning of the parable first.

PARABLE OF THE GREAT SUPPER (Luke 14:16-24). "When you give a dinner, do not ask people you know, because they will be likely to invite you back. But when you give a dinner, invite those who cannot repay you. You will be blessed at the resurrection of the just" (Luke 14:12-14).

LOST SHEEP (Matthew 18:12, 13). "The Son of Man has come to save that which was lost" (Matthew 18:11).

FORGIVENESS (Matthew 18:23-34). "I do not say to you, up to seven times, but up to seventy times seven" (Matthew 18:22).

FIG TREE (Mark 13:28). "Now learn this parable from the fig tree" (Mark 13:28).

Jesus provided a cue for his audience to pay attention for the parable about to be told.

Ask a Question

Another excellent technique to grab the attention of your audience is to ask questions. This is effective for any type of presentation or sermon and is exemplified best by Jesus.

"To what shall we liken the kingdom of God? Or with what parable shall we picture it?" (Mark 4:30).

This is a good example of asking a question to indicate that a parable is imminent (Mark 4:31, 32).

Transitioning Out of the Story

It seems like the default structure of a children's story session is to tell a story and then say, "The moral of the story is ..." However, Jesus provided numerous methods to smoothly transition from a story to its lesson.

State the Moral

On several occasions Jesus simply stated the point of the parable.

> "So My Father will do to you if each of you, from his heart, does not forgive his brother his trespasses" (Matthew 18:35).

"So you also, when you see these things happening, know that the kingdom of God is near" (Luke 21:31).

"Likewise, I say to you, there is joy in the presence of the angels of God over one sinner who repents" (Luke 15:10).

In these examples Jesus transitioned directly from the parable to the conclusion. A variation of this approach is to say, "That's when I learned ..." followed by the moral. There is a subtle difference in wording between "What I want you to learn . . ." and "That's when I learned ..."; it is the difference between preaching to the audience and revealing the result of your own experience, a form of testimony. Another way to state the moral is by saying, "This story reminds me of a Bible verse." Let the Bible reveal the point of the story.

Ask a Question

As with introducing a story, questioning is an effective way to conclude a story. At the end of the parable of the good Samaritan (Luke 10:30-35), Jesus asked, "Which of these three do you think was the neighbor to him who fell among thieves?" (Luke 10:36).

After telling the parable of the persistent widow (Luke 18:2-5), Jesus asked, "When the Son of Man comes, will He truly find faith on the earth?" (Luke 18:8).

Following the parable of the wicked vineyard workers (Matthew 21:33-39), Jesus asked, "When the owner of the vineyard comes, what will he do to those workers?" (Matthew 21:40).

No Moral Presented

Jesus told a few parables where He publicly told the parable and privately revealed the meaning. In Mark's version of the parable of the sower, Jesus simply started with "Listen!" (Mark 4:3) and ended with "He who has ears to hear, let him hear" (Mark 4:9). Matthew and Luke end their versions of the parable the same way.

In the parable of the barren fig tree (Luke 13:6-9), the parable ends with "But if not, after that you can cut it down" (v9). The next verse? "Now He was teaching in one of the synagogues on the Sabbath" (v10). This parable has neither an introduction nor a concluding moral. This technique is useful because it requires the audience to use their cognitive abilities to contemplate the moral and how the lesson story might be applied.

Including Introductions and Conclusions

For many of the parables, Jesus provided an introduction and a conclusion.

Matthew 21:28 - "What do you think?"
- Parable of the Two Sons

Matthew 21:31 - "Which of the two did the will of the father?"

Mark 13:34 - "It is like a man going to a far country."
- Watching for the Master's Return

Mark 13:37 - "I say to all: Watch!"

Matthew 19:30 - "Many who are first will be last, and the last first."

STORY SECRETS FROM SCRIPTURE

- Parable of the Vineyard Workers

Matthew 20:16 - "So the last will be first, and the first last."

Luke 12:35 - "Be dressed and ready; keep your lamps burning."

- Faithful and Evil Servants

Luke 12:40 - "Therefore be ready, for the Son of Man is coming at an hour when you do not expect Him."

Variety

Jesus told us through the apostle John, "If you love Me, keep My commandments" (John 14:15). John wrote in one of his letters, "By this we know Him, that we keep His commandments" (1 John 2:3). In Revelation, amidst the prophetic imagery and church history, John further wrote, "Blessed are those who keep His commandments, for they shall have access to the tree of life and may enter the gates into the city" (Revelation 22:14).

Obedience to God is essential. In fact, many of the children's stories I hear at churches center around one theme: *obedience*. Often the stories follow this basic outline:

INITIAL SITUATION
A mother tells her children to stay away from a forbidden place.

COMPLICATIONS
One day, while the mother is gone, the children go to the forbidden place.

ACTION
While in the forbidden place, one of the children is injured. The other child runs home and tells the mother.

RESULT

HOW JESUS SHARED PARABLES

The mother retrieves the injured child from the forbidden place and provides medical care.
FINAL SITUATION
The children learned to always obey the mother.

You can probably recall several stories based on this plot. Whether the "forbidden place" is the jungle, the abandoned house across the street, an activity or a body of water, these cautionary tales share the same moral, often presented after a hard transition between the end of the story and the sharing of the moral. Stories based on this plot rarely hold interest for children because the plot is predictable. No unexpected complications and surprises to captivate and delight are included. Children of the early elementary school age are fascinated by justice, which can include a resolution of a situation. Jesus said, "I desire mercy, not sacrifice" (Matthew 12:7), and a children's story is an opportunity to share the many themes Jesus introduced.

Why couldn't the Final Situation be one of these?
- The child who was not injured sought help for the other child.
- The mother came as quickly as she could because she loved the child.
- The family said a prayer of thanks because everything turned out alright.
- The injured child realized that her mother loved her.
- The children learned to rely on each other for support during difficult times.

Like these alternate Final Situations, obedience is not the only theme of the Bible. Salvation, mercy, love, forgiveness can be easily seen throughout the Bible from Genesis to Revelation. For this book, I conducted a search of key themes in the Bible via online searches ("key themes in the Bible"), recalled several verses that include descriptions of God (Exodus 34:6, 7) and Christian growth (Philippians 4:8, 2 Peter 1:5-7) and quickly scanned several books of the Bible for themes. See pages 110-111 for my complete list of themes. Below are a few from the list:

Abundance	Endurance	Faith	Faithfulness
Freedom	Generosity	Justice	Kindness
Messiah	Overcoming	Redeemed	Righteousness

Jesus told several parables as recorded by Matthew, Mark and Luke. These parables included three central themes: the kingdom of heaven, salvation and Christian behavior.

Another characteristic of the parables of Jesus is that He only associated one point to a specific parable. Consider the parable of the lost coin (Luke 15:8,9):

> A woman had ten silver coins, but she lost one. She immediately lit a lamp, swept the house, and carefully looked everywhere until she found the coin. After she found the coin, she called her neighbors and friends together, saying, "Rejoice with me, for I have found what was lost."

Jesus concluded with, "Likewise, I say to you, there is joy in the presence of the angels of God over one sinner who repents" (Luke 15:10).

Jesus could have said added, "Take care not to lose what you have" and "Share the good news with others." But to the original hearers, each of Jesus' parables had one meaning as recorded in the Bible. Modern professional communication training advocates this same principle: a short presentation of 3-5 minutes should have one point or call-to-action.

The Kingdom of Heaven

From the beginning of His earthly ministry Jesus said, "Repent, for the kingdom of heaven is at hand," He continually spoke of His kingdom, the kingdom of heaven, the kingdom of God. Through a variety of parables and similes, Jesus described different aspects of the kingdom.

CONTRAST

Jesus used contrast between two elements to illustrate readiness for the kingdom of heaven and the nature of the kingdom. The parable of the ten virgins and the wheat and the tares are told in Chapter 3. The parable of the fishing net is another example of comparison/contrast.

> The kingdom of heaven is like a fishing net that was put out from the boat into the lake. Every kind of fish was gathered into the net. When the net was full, the boat returned to shore. The good fish were gathered into containers, but the bad were thrown away. Matthew 13:47, 48.

STORY SECRETS FROM SCRIPTURE

TOTAL COMMITMENT

Through parables, Jesus described the total commitment required to be part of the kingdom of God.

> The kingdom of heaven is like a treasure hidden in a field. A man stumbled upon a treasure in a field and then re-hid it. He was so excited that he sold everything he owned and bought the field. Matthew 13:44.

> The kingdom of heaven is like a merchant who searched for pearls. When he found one of great beauty that was very expensive, the merchant sold everything to buy the pearl. Matthew 13:45, 46.

EXPANSIVE

Jesus illustrated the expansive nature of the kingdom of God.

> The kingdom of God is like a man who scattered seed on the ground. Day and night while the man slept and worked, the seed sprouted and grew, but the man did not know how. All he could see was that the earth yielded the crops by itself: first the tender shoots of the plant, then the bud and after that the full grain. When the man saw the ripened grain, he immediately harvested the field. Mark 4:26-29.

> The kingdom of God is like a mustard seed. Before it is planted, it is one of the smallest seeds around. Once planted, it grows until it becomes greater than all other herbs and even has branches where birds can build nests in the shade provided by the plant. Mark 4:30-32.

> The kingdom of God is like yeast. A woman took some yeast and mixed it into the other ingredients. The entire

dough was affected by the yeast and rose until doubled in size. Luke 13:20, 21.

AVAILABLE TO ALL

Jesus showed that the kingdom of God is available to all who choose to accept the invitation.

> A landowner went out very early in the morning and hired laborers for his vineyard at the rate of one denarius for the day. Around 9:00 a.m. the landowner went out again and hired more workers, "Go into my vineyard and I will give you whatever is right." At noon and at 3:00 p.m. he once again hired additional workers for his vineyard. Finally, around 5:00 p.m. the landowner still needed workers. He found some who had been waiting for jobs all day. He said, "Why are you standing here idle? Come work for me today, and I will give you whatever is right."
>
> At the end of the day, the landowner paid all the workers. He gave the last workers - who had only worked about an hour—one denarius. He gave those who had come throughout the day one denarius each as well. When the first workers—who had been there all day—received their pay, it was also one denarius per worker, as promised. The first workers said, "Look, we've been here all day. Is it fair to give us and those who only worked a short time the same amount?" The landowner replied, "I did not harm you. You agreed to work for one denarius. Take what is yours and leave. It is not your business how I spend my money. I can give everyone who works for me whatever I want." Matthew 20:1-16.

Other Themes

STORY SECRETS FROM SCRIPTURE

SALVATION

A man gave a great banquet and invited many. He sent his servant to those who had been invited, "Come, for all things are now ready." But all of them began to make excuses.

"I have to go look at a piece of land I bought. Please excuse me," said one.

Another said, "I just purchased five yoke of oxen and I need to test them. Please excuse me."

Still another said, "I have recently married, so I cannot come."

The servant returned and told all to his master. The man hosting the banquet became angry and gave new instructions to the servant: "Go out quickly into the streets and lanes of the city. Bring the poor, the maimed, the blind, and the lame."

The servant came back soon afterward, "Master, I have done as you ordered, and there is still room."

The host said, "Go out again into the highways and hedges to bring in more guests, so that my house will be full." Luke 14:16-24.

HOW JESUS SHARED PARABLES

FAITH

Imagine what would happen if you went to a friend in the middle of the night and said, "Friend, lend me three loaves of bread. An old friend traveling through just showed up, and I don't have a thing on hand."

The friend answers from his bed, "Don't bother me. The door's locked; my children are all down for the night; I can't get up to give you anything." Let me tell you, even if he won't get up because he's a friend, if you stand your ground, knocking and waking all the neighbors, he'll finally get up and get you whatever you need. Luke 11:5-8MSG

DOING THE FATHER'S WILL

A man had two sons. He came to the first and said, "Son, go out and work today in my vineyard."

The son answered, "I will not go," but later regretted his decision and went to work in the vineyard.

The man then came to his other son and said the same thing, "Son, go out and work today in my vineyard."

The son answered, "I will go, sir," but he did not go. Matthew 21:28-30.

THE TRUE SHEPHERD

If someone does not enter the sheepfold by the door, but instead climbs up some other way, he is a thief or a robber. He who enters by the door is the shepherd of the sheep. The sheep know his voice, and they will respond to him. When he leads them, they will follow. But they will not follow a stranger. The sheep will flee from him, because they do not know the voice of strangers. John 10:1-5.

SELFISHNESS

The fields of a rich man produced an abundant harvest. He thought to himself, what should I do since I don't have any more room to store my crops? I will do this: I will tear down my barns and builder larger ones. There I will store all my crops and my goods. I will say to myself, "Friend, you have provided abundantly for your future. Now you can take it easy, eating and drinking and enjoying life to its fullest."

But God said to him, "You are a fool! This night you will die. What good will those things be to you then?" Luke 12:16-20.

PLEADING FOR OTHERS

A man planted a fig tree in his vineyard. He came to the tree expecting fruit, but he found none. He said to the manager of his vineyard, "Look, for three years I have been coming here with the hope of finding figs on this tree, but the result is always the same—no fruit. Cut down this tree; it is just wasting useful space in the vineyard."

But the manager said, "Sir, leave it this year also. I will improve the irrigation and fertilize around it. Then, if it bears fruit, fantastic! If not, then you can cut it down." Luke 13:6-9.

Jesus effectively connected with His audiences during His earthly ministry because, as Matthew wrote, "Jesus did not say anything to the crowd without using a parable" (Matthew 13:34

HOW JESUS SHARED PARABLES

NIV). Jesus shared a full range of dimensions of the love of God through the illustrations He used. These same approaches of using stories and varied themes can also be applied to children's stories today.

Summary

In this chapter you learned about how Jesus shared parables:
1. Introduce parables using techniques such as sharing the moral or asking a question.
2. Transition out of a story using techniques such as asking a question, stating the moral, or simply ending the story.
3. Include both introductions and conclusions to state and restate a moral or reinforce key points of the story.
4. Use a variety of themes and techniques when telling stories.

STORY SECRETS FROM SCRIPTURE

5.

FINDING STORIES

In this chapter you will learn about:
- How to find stories from your own experiences.
- Guidelines for choosing stories.
- Stories from my life (including my family) illustrating the five-part structure.

Stories abound everywhere. Many books have been written which contain stories that have been used for children's story time. A few of these story sources include:
- The Bible
- Bedtime story collections
- Stories from missionaries
- Stories on Facebook (shared and re-shared)
- Stories heard in other churches

While these are solid sources of material, the fact that these stories have been published means other storytellers and children may be familiar with the stories. I have heard stories repeated from time to time. If you wait ten years before sharing again, your audience of children will change, making it safe to retell a story. Rather than relying on a common body of stories known to many, it is better to conduct research to find stories that are less well known or to search your own experiences to find stories.

Find Your Own Stories

The best source of stories for you to tell is you. Your own stories are only familiar to those you have shared them with. From the perspective of other listeners, these are fresh stories that they have never heard. You can also be assured that your stories are unlikely to be used by others, like having a private library only available to you. No one knows your personal experiences better than you.

Family is also a good source of stories. These may be stories that you have heard again and again. Two of the stories in the next section feature my father and his siblings when they were children. I heard these stories many times as a child. Because you are familiar with your own stories, it is easier to recall the details and structure. As a result, you may have more enjoyment telling your own stories than those you discover from other sources.

FINDING STORIES

Guidelines

In thinking about stories for children, keep these guidelines in mind.

Avoid offending parents. Years ago, I wrote a fable version of the Good Samaritan parable using animals as speaking characters. From the standpoint of fables, it was a solid story. However, because animals don't speak, some parents were not pleased when I shared this story for the children's story during a worship service. I should have simply retold the parable of the Good Samaritan using people, like Jesus did.

Do not frighten children. A visitor to a church I attended told the following to a group of children assembled for the children's story: "Boys and girls, did you know that there are people who do not believe like we do? One day mean men will come through the back door of the church and kill your parents. They might kill you too or take you away to become slaves."

Because persecution of Christians has existed and continues to exist (especially in other countries), the essence of the message shared by the visiting storyteller was true. However, these "truths" were not well-received by parents or the children who began crying at the thought of losing their parents.

Use age-appropriate stories. Stories that pass the first two guidelines also need to be appropriate developmentally for children, as discussed in Chapter 1. Children need literal, concrete concepts, not abstract ones.

During my second semester of college, as a declared business major, I let my mind wander during a lecture on works-in-progress (Accounting 102) and envisioned myself working in a cubicle on accounts receivables for the rest of my life, a future I found undesirable. I immediately changed my major to behavioral science (a mix of psychology, sociology, and social work) because I had been enjoying my class in family studies.

This story about my career goals and aspirations has an appropriate audience, but it is not children. Children don't understand professional accounting, can't conceive of how college works, and won't appreciate the uncertainty I experienced in college.

Add meaning. Children's stories should be more than just an entertaining interlude before a sermon or other events. Stories are most effective when they teach a spiritual lesson, like the parables of Jesus. Both children and adults will benefit from this approach.

Two approaches to finding a story include starting with a story or starting with a moral. When starting with a story, try to find the teaching point. As a teenager fleeing during the Korean War, my father-in-law had an encounter with an angel. This is a great story that I like to share. My moral for this story is that God will protect you when you trust Him. When starting with a moral, an easy way to develop a story from this perspective is to align the story's teaching point with a program's theme or sermon topic. Children will learn from the story, and adults will hear the same theme twice, in the story and the sermon.

Ways to Find Stories

Unless you have been keeping a journal or diary since childhood, recovering stories from your memory will require mental time travel.

RELATIONSHIPS

Often the best stories to illustrate spiritual themes involve relationships. Jesus told parables about fathers and sons, masters

and servants, and interactions between individuals. Use these prompts to get story ideas about relationships:
- When you helped a sibling or a sibling helped you
- When a sibling did not help you or you got in trouble
- When your parents showed mercy to you
- When your parents helped you with a problem
- Playground encounters—good and bad
- Friends with whom you played
- Acquaintances who picked fights or caused trouble
- A time you had to deliver bad news
- A time you and others couldn't agree
- A time you fought (literally or figuratively) with someone

PERSONAL EXPERIENCES

Part of growing up includes living in the world. These prompts may also generate some ideas:
- Holiday experiences
- First times
- Experiences with elements such as wind, fire, and water
- A time you were lost
- A decision you made with unexpected outcomes

MAPS AND PHOTOS

Looking at old photos of your family and experiences may bring back memories from which you can generate story ideas. Maps are also an excellent visual. Draw a map of your childhood neighborhood, school, and house to help you recall stories. In my childhood neighborhood I broke my arm, my brother lost his front tooth in a bicycle accident, I took my first piano lessons, I "drove" my parents' new car into a ditch when I was three years old, I adopted a neighbor's dog, I made friends, and I lost friends. If you moved frequently you will have sets of different stories from each neighborhood. A map of locations (cities, states, and countries) is also useful.

THEMES IN THE BIBLE

From the list of key themes in the Bible (pp110-111), select a theme and reflect back on your experiences to see if any story ideas reveal themselves. For example, if the theme is *abundance*, was there a time in your life—or someone you know—when everyone was satisfied? If the theme is *freedom*, tell about a time you were prevented from a certain desirable course of action. Perhaps school or work prevented you from engaging in leisure activities, or a time you were released from a debt or an obligation.

Recording Stories

When you think of stories that might work for a children's story, write down the ideas. Today we have numerous ways to record thoughts: note applications on phones, word processing documents, spreadsheets, notebooks, journals, self-adhesive notes, and many more. Capturing story ideas in one of these formats will make it easier to find stories from your collection to tell.

What you write down may depend on the time you have available and your need to recall information. It may be enough to recall a story from "My brother kicking the wall with my boot," or a story may need the framework of the five-part structure discussed in previous chapters. You can also write out full versions of stories, but these should not be used when telling your stories (see Chapter 7).

Conclusion (Moral)

For each story, follow the structure outline I have been using throughout this book.
- Initial situation
- Complications
- Action
- Result
- Final Situation

Two additional elements should also be added: the moral or point of the story and a text. Regardless of how you transition out of the story, summarizing the spiritual idea or moral will help you to complete the story. Sharing a text as part of the transition out of a story reinforces the moral.

My Stories

Following are five true stories. One was shared by a friend, two are from my father's childhood, and two are from my own experiences.

STORY SECRETS FROM SCRIPTURE

Mud on the Carpet

INITIAL SITUATION
Andrea and Billy played quietly while their parents visited in a different room.

COMPLICATIONS
While playing, Andrea and Billy knocked over a plant.

ACTION
They attempted to clean it up with water, but created a large mud stain on the carpet.

RESULT
They never told their parents or the owner of the house.

FINAL SITUATION
The owner had to have professionals clean the carpet.

CONCLUSION
Ask for help when you get in trouble.

TEXT
Luke 8:24 - They came to Jesus and awoke Him, saying, "Master, Master, we are perishing!" Jesus arose and rebuked the wind and the raging sea. Then there was calm.

The Smith and Johnson families were invited by the Petersons for lunch on the weekend. The Smith family had one daughter, Andrea, who was nine years old. The Johnsons had a son, Billy, who was eight years old. Both Andrea and Billy came to lunch with their parents. The Petersons had a child too, but it was a newborn infant.

After a delicious lunch, the children were excused to play quietly in a separate room while the grownups talked. Billy brought his toy building blocks with him, and for a while Andrea and Billy sat on the floor building various objects and playing with the items created. Andrea and her family had just returned from a trip, so she said, "Billy, let's build airplanes and pretend to take a trip in the room." Billy agreed, and they quickly assembled airplanes from the building blocks.

Both children taxied their planes down the runway and then lifted them into the air with their arms. The children wandered around the room pretending to fly their planes. As Billy was concluding his pretend trip he brought the plane in for a landing. As the plane was approaching the runway, Billy's arm brushed against a plant on a stand. The plant fell to the floor. The pot was not broken, but quite a bit of dirt was dumped onto the carpet in the living room, where the children were playing.

"Oh no," said Billy, "what are we going to do?" He started to cry.

"Stop crying," Andrea said, "Let's just clean it up ourselves. I don't want to tell Mom and Dad."

"Yeah," said Billy.

Both Andrea and Billy went into the bathroom. They took handfuls of toilet paper and wet it in the sink. Then they carried their cleaning supplies into the living room. Billy put the plant back on the stand and scooped up as much dirt as possible. They both knelt and began wiping up the dirt with their wet toilet paper.

"That doesn't look too bad," said Andrea.

Just then Billy's mom said, "Children, it's time to go!" Billy and Andrea picked up their toys, said good-bye to the Petersons and left.

Later, Mrs. Peterson called Andrea's mom and said, "I found a mess in the living room after you left. It looks like the children tried to clean up after a plant was knocked over. If they had let me know, we could have let the dirt dry and just vacuum it up.

STORY SECRETS FROM SCRIPTURE

However, now there's a mud stain, and I have to have the carpets cleaned."

Boys and girls, did you know that many times we are like Andrea and Billy? Things are going along well and then, when we get it trouble, we tried to solve it ourselves. If you find yourself in a situation like Andrea and Billy, ask your parents for help. Jesus wants to help us, but we need to ask Him for help.

Jim and the Chickens

INITIAL SITUATION
Jim's responsibility was to feed the chickens every day. For entertainment, he used a broom to fight with the roosters.

COMPLICATIONS
One day Jim was sick, so his sister Lois had to feed the chickens.

ACTION
Because no one told Lois about the broom, the roosters attacked her. She panicked and ran out of the chicken coop, and the chickens escaped.

RESULT
Jim had to put all the chickens back into the coop while Lois recovered from the attack and her anxiety.

FINAL SITUATION
Decades later, she is still afraid of birds.

CONCLUSION
Warn others of potential danger.

TEXT
Ezekiel 3:17 - I have made you a watchman; therefore, hear a word from My mouth, and give them warning from Me.

Jim and Lois lived on a farm with their parents. Jim was eight years old and Lois was nine years old when this story happened.

FINDING STORIES

On a farm everyone has chores, and one of Jim's responsibilities was to feed the chickens every day. The chickens lived in a pen, usually called a chicken coop. What do chickens lay every day? That's right—eggs! In addition to gathering the eggs to take to his mom, Jim also fed the chickens and made sure they had water to drink.

There were not only egg-laying chickens in the pen, but there were also two roosters. Roosters like to protect their chickens and tend to fight. Well, Jim liked to take a broom and fight with the roosters. Whenever the roosters saw someone coming to the pen, they got excited and started jumping around. By the time Jim opened the door to the chicken coop, the roosters were ready to fight. But Jim had his broom and was able to protect himself while he fed the chickens and gathered the eggs. This happened every day.

It happened one day that Jim was sick. He had a fever and his mom said, "Jim, you're going to stay in bed today and get some rest. I'll send Lois to feed the chickens."

Jim and Lois's mom said, "Lois, since Jim is sick, go out to the chicken coop. Feed the chickens and gather the eggs in this basket."

Lois said, "Yes ma'am," and immediately went out to the chicken coop. The rooster saw her coming and began to get excited. By the time she opened the door, the roosters were right there at the entrance and attacked her. No one told her about the rooster or the broom or what happened every day at feeding time. The roosters became excited, and this caused all the chickens to get excited. So, they attacked Lois too.

Lois ran out of the chicken coop but forgot to close the door. All the chickens escaped into the yard. Later in the day Jim felt

STORY SECRETS FROM SCRIPTURE

better, and his mom gave him the chore of returning all the chickens and rooster to their home, the chicken coop. After that day Lois was afraid of birds, and she is still afraid of birds.

What are some lessons we can learn from this story? All of those are true, but the one thing I would like you to think about today is this ... If you see that someone is going to be in trouble, warn them about what is happening. Do you know Jesus is coming soon? People all around us are in trouble. They are fighting with Satan, and we need to let them know how to win.

Olive and the Woodstove

INITIAL SITUATION
Olive was instructed to keep the wet clothes away from the wood stove while laundry dried. Lois and Jim played outside. They found a box used to mix cement and turned it into a boat on the pond. Olive watched them through the window.

COMPLICATIONS
When Olive saw what they were doing, she ran outside to tell them to return to shore. But then she had to check on the laundry. She eventually forgot about the clothes drying around the wood stove because she was focused on Jim and Lois. The clothes caught on fire.

ACTION
When their father noticed smoke coming from the house, he quickly ran into the house with a bucket of water and doused the burning clothes.

RESULT
Some of the clothes were lost ...

FINAL SITUATION
... but the house was saved.

CONCLUSION
Focus on your work and don't worry about others.

FINDING STORIES

TEXT
Hebrews 13:5 - Let your conduct be without covetousness; be content with such things as you have.

Olive, Lois and Jim were siblings. The difference between Olive (the oldest) and Jim (the youngest) was three years. They were very close as children, and often played together. As this story was set in a different time, you might have some difficulty imagining: there were no washing machines and dryers like most of us have today. The clothes had to be washed by hand and then hung up to dry. Most times, if the weather was nice, the clothes were hung outside to dry as the wind blew and the sun shone down. When this story occurred, the weather was not particularly nice, so the clothes were hung up around a wood stove inside the house.

Olive's mom told her, "Olive, I want you to stay inside and make sure these clothes don't touch the wood stove and catch on fire."

Olive said, "Yes ma'am!"

While Olive stayed inside watching the clothes, she occasionally looked out the window where Jim and Lois were playing. During their play they found a wooden box their father used to mix cement. As a result, the seams of the box were sealed. Jim said to Lois, "Let's see if this will float in the pond." Jim and Lois carried the box to the pond and discovered that it floated!

Lois said, "Let's get in the box!" Jim and Lois climbed into the box and floated along the shore of the small pond.

While all this activity was going on, Olive knocked on the window, but Jim and Lois did not hear her. Olive, the oldest of the three siblings, fancied herself to be a junior parent and often bossed Jim and Lois around. Olive looked at the clothes hanging around the woodstove and then she quickly ran outside. "Jim and Lois," she yelled, "get out of the pond and put that box back before Daddy comes home. You're going to be in big trouble."

Then Olive ran back in to check on the clothes. Everything was alright. Olive ran outside again. She warned Jim and Lois, "You're going to get in trouble." Olive was close to the door. Then she moved to the edge of the pond, "Don't blame me if Daddy spanks you."

As their father was walking back to the house from the barn, he noticed two things: he saw his children playing at the edge of the pond and he laughed. Then he looked towards the house and noticed smoke wafting out through the open door. He stopped laughing. He quickly ran to a bucket, filled it with water from the pond, and entered the house. Sure enough, there was a fire. He tossed the water and put out the fire.

Some clothes were lost, but the house was saved.

This was a true story that happened many years ago. My dad is Jim, and his older sisters are Lois and Olive. My dad told this story to me many times when I was growing up, especially when I was more focused on what others were doing rather than on myself.

The Abandoned Truck

INITIAL SITUATION
My friends and I loved to ride our bikes around an abandoned house site in the neighborhood.

COMPLICATIONS
We came across what appeared to be an abandoned toy truck.

ACTIONS
Just for fun we decided to kick the truck.

FINDING STORIES

RESULT
Eventually the truck was destroyed and we all returned to our homes.

FINAL SITUATION
Somehow my mom already knew about this situation, and I had to pay for the truck out of my allowance money.

CONCLUSION
Don't take or use what doesn't belong to you.

TEXT
Matthew 7:12 - Whatever you want men to do to you, do also to them, for this is the Law and the Prophets.

When I was growing up, there was an abandoned house site in my neighborhood where we used to play. Years earlier a tornado came through the neighborhood and destroyed a house. We loved to ride our bikes around the vacant lot. On one occasion, while we were playing at this abandoned house site, we came across a shiny, brand new toy fire truck. It was a hook-and-ladder truck, so it was long. It had a ladder you could crank up and down.

An older boy in our group kicked the truck, and it flipped over. Then another boy kicked it. Then I kicked it. I really wasn't thinking, but I just followed along with the actions of the others. We kept kicking the toy fire truck until it was destroyed. A few minutes later we all went to our homes.

When I walked in the kitchen from the garage, my mom said to me, "Douglas," which she only used when I was in trouble, "tell me about the fire truck at the place where you like to ride bikes." Somehow, my mom already knew what had happened! I explained to her what happened, and she said to me, "Would you want someone doing that to one of your toys if you accidentally left it out somewhere?"

"No," I said.

Mom made me take money from my allowance and pay for a new fire truck for the child. This was an important lesson for me to be respectful of the property of others. It says in Matthew, "Treat others the same way you want to be treated."

Missionary Goldfish

INITIAL SITUATION
A missionary visiting from Asia bought some fish to use for a children's story.

COMPLICATIONS
But he left the fish at the ministry when he returned to Asia. The fish could not stay at the ministry.

ACTION
My daughter brought the fish home, but I ended up taking care of them.

RESULT
Though tempted to release the fish into a local pond I decided to keep the fish.

FINAL SITUATION
Taking care of the fish has been enjoyable.

CONCLUSION
We should take care of even the smallest of God's creation.

TEXT
Luke 12:6 - Not one sparrow is forgotten by God.

Not too long ago a missionary from Asia visited us here at our church. He also visited some other churches. He had planned to tell a children's story and wanted to use fish as part of his story. He went to Walmart and bought six goldfish and a small fish bowl. However, he decided to tell a different story.

So, the missionary left the fish at the ministry office and returned to Asia. The fish stayed here, in our town. Now, the people who work in the ministry office travel a lot because they must go to Asia and check on the missionaries. Who would take care of the fish when no one was in the office? My daughter worked in the office, and she said, "I'll take the fish home and take care of them." Everyone was happy because the fish had found a new home.

Except me. I was not happy. Why was I unhappy? Because I knew Erika would not feed the fish for long nor would she want to clean the tank when the water became cloudy. These were not Erika's first fish! She had tried to care for fish before, and the same thing happened. For a few days, Erika took care of the fish, but then she stopped feeding them because she was busy with work and school.

At first, I thought, how can I get rid of these fish?

Someone told me, "One of your neighbors has a pond." I thought about sneaking them into the pond. Soon after, I went to a Chinese restaurant where there is a nice fountain and large goldfish in the entryway of the restaurant. I thought about "accidentally" putting the fish in there. It would be easy to do, I thought, just put them in a water bottle or a bag and whoops!

But then I read in the Desire of Ages, "He whose word of power upheld the worlds would stoop to relieve a wounded bird." I also thought about the text in Luke 12:6, "Not one sparrow is forgotten by God."

I thought, "If God cares about sparrows, He also cares about goldfish."

STORY SECRETS FROM SCRIPTURE

We still have the goldfish at our house. They now live in a larger tank and have fish toys. The fish have learned when it's feeding time, and it is fun to watch them follow me if I move around near feeding time. They are very happy. I am too!

Summary

In this chapter you learned about ways to find stories:
1. Use stories from your own experiences because they are unique and have a personal meaning.
2. Take care to avoid offending parents and frightening children when selecting a story. Use age-appropriate stories.
3. When planning a story using the five-part structure, include the conclusion (moral) as well as a supporting text.
4. Review the stories of others or lists of themes and topics for ideas.

6.

ORIENTED TIMES THREE

In this chapter you will learn about:
- Ways to orient your audience to the story.
- How to use different points-of-view.
- Considerations for telling stories from different perspectives.

When my daughter was nine years old she had a bicycle accident. She was wearing a helmet, but her face hit the pavement. Blood was everywhere. She briefly lost consciousness (for about two seconds). Three stitches and a few hours later she was back on her bike.

Whenever someone loses consciousness, is suspected of having a concussion, or otherwise seems disoriented, medical professionals will typically ask about three things to check the patient's awareness of their surroundings:
- What is your name?
- Where are you?
- What date (or day) is it?

If patients can answer all three questions correctly, they are *oriented times three*, in other words, fully oriented to their surroundings.

Orientation in Storytelling

Maintaining your audience's attention as you tell a story is critical. Stories often involve events, people, and places from the past. After all, something happening right now—in real time—doesn't yet have a Final Situation, as we have already explored. If your audience can follow the people, locations, and times of the story, they will be more engaged and more likely to listen—or at least less likely to become distracted.

An example from the Old Testament that sets the stage for a series of stories is Genesis 18:1: "Then the Lord appeared to [Abraham] by the terebinth trees of Mamre, as he was sitting in the tent door in the heat of the day."
- **Person:** The Lord, Abraham
- **Place:** by the terebinth trees
- **Time:** hottest part of the day

Another example that specifies a general group of people is found in Esther 1:2, 3: "In those days when King Ahasuerus sat on the throne of his kingdom, which was in Shushan the citadel, in the third year of his reign, he made a feast for all his officials and servants."

- **Person:** King Ahasuerus, officials and servants
- **Place:** the citadel in Shushan
- **Time:** third year of the king's reign

An example from the New Testament is Matthew 2:1: "Now after Jesus was born in Bethlehem of Judea in the days of Herod the king, behold, wise men from the East came to Jerusalem."

- **Person:** Jesus, wise men
- **Place:** Bethlehem, the East
- **Time:** in the days of Herod

One more example, from Acts, shows how these elements of orientation can be summarized into a short sentence. Acts 3:1: "Now Peter and John went up together to the temple at the hour of prayer, the ninth hour."

- **Person:** Peter and John
- **Place:** the temple
- **Time:** the ninth hour

Place can refer to a specific geographic location or a general area. *Time* can be a specific period of history (date) or a time of the day (e.g., night, sunrise, noon, etc.). Knowledge of these details makes these stories more memorable and vivid. Oriented times three for stories allows the storyteller to answer these questions:

- Where are we?
- Who is there?
- When did this occur?

The best part of the story to provide orientation details to your audience is during the Initial Situation, where details relevant to the setup of the story are told. You may have found yourself telling a story to someone only to remember a critical person, place, or time element. These are critical, especially if the story outcome depends on these details.

Point-of-View

Point-of-view refers to how the story is told. It answers the question, "Who is telling this story?" Four primary points-of-view are used in fictional and non-fictional storytelling: first-person, second-person, third-person (omniscient and limited).

First-Person

The first-person point-of-view occurs when the storyteller is sharing about themselves or is relating a story on behalf of a character in the story. For example, "I went to the grocery store and purchased a bottle of water. We drank it during the day." If storytellers are sharing stories from their own lives, this is most likely the point-of-view adopted.

The book of Nehemiah is written in the first-person point-of-view. Nehemiah was a Jew who served the king in the citadel of Shushan. Nehemiah was profoundly affected by the news that the wall of the city of Jerusalem was in ruins. The king observed Nehemiah's sadness and authorized him to travel to Jerusalem and coordinate rebuilding efforts. Nehemiah wrote, "So I came to Jerusalem and was there three days" (Nehemiah 2:11). Throughout the book, Nehemiah maintained the first-person point-of-view and ended with a prayer, "Remember me, O my God, for good" (Nehemiah 13:31).

Revelation is also written in the first-person point-of-view. John wrote, "I was in the Spirit on the Lord's Day, and I heard behind me a loud voice, as of a trumpet" (Revelation 1:10). John wrote about the things he saw in vision, but also interacted with angels and elders throughout the book and was affected by what he saw. "I wept much, because no one was found worthy to open the scroll, or to look at it. But one of the elders said to me, 'Do not weep'" (Revelation 5:4). "Now I, John, saw and heard these things. When I heard and saw, I fell to worship before the feet of the angel who showed me these things. He said to me, 'See that you do not do that. For I am your fellow servant. Worship God'" (Revelation 22:8, 9).

Second-Person

The second-person point-of-view occurs when I am describing what someone else did as though I am speaking to that person. For example, "You walk into a room and jump when someone surprises you." This point-of-view is most effective when helping your audience to become immersed in a situation. For example, "Imagine you are descending a set of stairs when you see a man emerging from the darkness." The second-person point-of-view is also used in investigations (ranging from court testimony to a mother admonishing a child). For example, "You ran into the room and knocked over the vase while waving your arms wildly."

Third-Person

The third-person point-of-view is the most frequently-used point-of-view. This is the traditional approach where the storyteller as narrator recounts events that occurred to someone else. For example, "He drove into the driveway and his wife opened the door."

Moses is considered the author of the Pentateuch, the first five books of the Jewish Torah and Christian Bible. Moses was not alive during the events of Genesis, but these were revealed to him through inspiration of the Holy Spirit. Thus, Moses simply wrote down what he likely observed through visions. He narrated the book of Genesis for future generations. Likewise, John Mark wrote the book of Mark, but he was not a disciple of Jesus. John Mark was a disciple of the apostles in the early Christian church. It is likely that his gospel narrative came about through the testimonies of Peter and others. Like Moses, John Mark simply narrated the events, but was not an eyewitness to them.

It is possible to experience events and still narrate them using the third-person point-of-view. Moses was an active participant of Exodus, especially as he was appointed by God to lead the children of Israel from Egypt to Canaan. However, Moses chose to narrate the story from a third-person point-of-view instead of the first-person. Matthew was a disciple of Jesus but narrated his gospel in the third-person.

Another aspect of the third-person point-of-view to consider is omniscient vs. limited. In the omniscient point-of-view, the narrator has insights into supernatural beings and the feelings of other characters in the story. We cannot know what others are thinking or feeling unless they translate thoughts and feelings into words and behaviors. In the limited point-of-view, the narrator simply recounts the events witnessed or told by others.

ORIENTED TIMES THREE

The book of Ruth is an example of the limited third-person point-of-view. Ruth was not a Jew by birth, but through a series of tragedies, returned with her former mother-in-law to Israel and eventually met and married Boaz, the great grandfather of David. The book of Ruth does not contain any insights from angels or direct messages from God.

In contrast, Job was written from the omniscient third-person point-of-view. After a brief Initial Situation to establish an orientation times three, we are immediately transported to heaven where, "the sons of God came to present themselves before the Lord, and Satan also came among them" (Job 1:6). God and Satan play important roles in the story of Job. In the last few chapters of Job, God speaks directly to Job, but no verses in the book suggest that Job had any awareness of his role in supernatural events.

Once you start telling a children's story using a particular point-of-view, continue from that point-of-view throughout the story. It can be confusing to switch back-and-forth from different viewpoints. If I was sharing a story about a tractor, I would not say, "Doug climbed onto the tractor and then I started driving."

Character Perspective

Another facet of storytelling related to point-of view is character perspective. It is likely that more than one character was involved in the stories you relate. Keeping in mind that we do not know the thoughts or feelings of others, could you tell a story from someone else's perspective other than your own? Would that change the story?

David

In 2 Samuel 11, the story followed this course:

INITIAL SITUATION
In the spring, King David sent his army to battle against Ammon. Only David remained in Jerusalem, where he saw a beautiful woman bathing. The woman was identified as Bathsheba, the wife of one of David's mighty men, Uriah.

COMPLICATIONS
David was intimate with Bathsheba, and she became pregnant.

ACTION
David called for Uriah to return and encouraged him to spend time with his wife. Uriah refused, out of loyalty to David.

RESULT
David had Uriah positioned where he would be killed during a fierce battle.

FINAL SITUATION
After an appropriate time of mourning, David married Bathsheba.

In 2 Samuel 12, the prophet Nathan came to David with a parable:

> There were two men in a city, a rich man and a poor man. The rich man had many flocks of sheep and herds of cattle. The poor man had only one lamb that he loved like a child. It ate at the table with the man's family, and he truly loved that lamb. When a visitor came to the rich man's house, the rich man did not want to kill one of his own sheep or cattle for the meal. Instead, he took the poor man's lamb and served it for dinner.

ORIENTED TIMES THREE

David's response to this parable is recorded in 2 Samuel 12:5, 6, "So David's anger was greatly aroused against the man, and he said to Nathan, 'As the Lord lives, the man who has done this shall surely die! He shall restore fourfold for the lamb, because he did this thing and because he had no pity.'"

Nathan chose to approach this delicate situation from the perspective of the victim, Uriah. Uriah was a servant of David. David was the king. The rich man in the parable represented David. Nathan could have started with an accusatory second-person point-of-view and recount for David the course of events. However, Nathan correctly predicted that telling this parable from the victim's perspective would arouse feelings that taking a more direct approach would not have accomplished.

Revisiting the Lost Sheep

Another example that is useful to examine from multiple perspectives is Jesus' parable of the lost sheep. In Chapter 2 I shared this as a simple example of the five-part story structure from the perspective of the shepherd: He lost a sheep, found it after searching, and rejoiced with his friends. However, what would the parable look like from the perspective of the sheep? This is my interpretation of the parable from the perspective of the sheep:

> As one of a flock of 100 sheep, a sheep wandered away from the flock while grazing in the fields. By the time he realized that he couldn't see the other sheep, he was stuck in a thicket. He bleated in a pitiful way as a call for help, but no one came. The shepherd did not return. The sheep eventually stopped crying and gave up trying to free himself. As darkness approached, the sheep

> heard singing and the sound of a familiar voice calling out his name. It was the shepherd! He had returned for the sheep. The sheep was freed from his bonds and returned on the shepherd's shoulders back to his home. The 100th sheep had returned to join the others.

This parable is part of a trio of parables to illustrate three conditions of lost sinners: those who know they are lost but can't find their way home (lost sheep), those who do not realize they are lost (lost coin), and those who know they are lost and are able to return (prodigal son). Below is a retelling of this parable from the perspective of the shepherd, like the original, but with more detail, in *Christ's Object Lessons*, pp187-190, by Ellen G. White.

> The shepherd who discovers that one of his sheep is missing does not look carelessly upon the flock that is safely housed, and say, "I have ninety and nine, and it will cost me too much trouble to go in search of the straying one. Let him come back, and I will open the door of the sheepfold, and let him in." No; no sooner does the sheep go astray than the shepherd is filled with grief and anxiety. He counts and recounts the flock. When he is sure that one sheep is lost, he slumbers not. He leaves the ninety and nine with the fold and goes in search of the straying sheep. The darker and more tempestuous the night and the more perilous the way, the greater is the shepherd's anxiety and the more earnest his search. He makes every effort to find that one lost sheep.

With what relief he hears in the distance its first faint cry. Following the sound, he climbs the steepest heights, he goes to the very edge of the precipice, at the risk of his own life. Thus, he searches, while the cry, growing fainter, tells him that his sheep is ready to die. At last his effort is rewarded; the lost is found. Then he does not scold it because it has caused him so much trouble. He does not drive it with a whip. He does not even try to lead it home. In his joy he takes the trembling creature upon his shoulders; if it is bruised and wounded, he gathers it in his arms, pressing it close to his bosom, that the warmth of his own heart may give it life. With gratitude that his search has not been in vain, he bears it back to the fold.

When the straying sheep is at last brought home, the shepherd's gratitude finds expression in melodious songs of rejoicing. He calls upon his friends and neighbors, saying unto them, "Rejoice with me; for I have found my sheep which was lost."

Daniel

The book of Daniel consists of two parts. The first half focuses on Daniel's experiences in Babylon. The second half focuses exclusively on prophecy. Chapter and verse divisions were not added until the Christian church was well-established. However, the chapter divisions of Daniel correspond perfectly to the stories—one story or prophecy for each chapter (the prophecy in Daniel 10-12 is an exception).

STORY SECRETS FROM SCRIPTURE

This table displays the point-of-view and character perspective for chapters 1-6 (listed individually) and chapters 7-12 (grouped).

Story	POV*	O/L*	Evidence for O or L (3RD Person)	Character Perspective
1 Captivity, diet, and education of Daniel	3RD	O	Supernatural involvement (vs 9, 17)	Daniel
2 The king's dream and Daniel's interpretation	3RD	O	Prophetic revelation (vs 19, 36)	The king
3 Image of gold	3RD	L	Observable conversations and actions	Daniel's friends
4 King's testimony	1ST (mostly)			The king
5 Fall of Babylon	3RD	O	Thoughts revealed (v22)	The king
6 Lions' den	3RD	O	Private conversations (v5) Thoughts revealed (v14) Private behavior (v18)	Daniel
7-12 Prophecies	1ST			Daniel
*POV = Point-of-view | O = Omniscient L = Limited				

As you plan your stories using the five-part structure, take some time to consider which point-of-view will be the most effective for your story and which character's perspective will be the most interesting. Even if you decide to use the first-person or third-person point-of-views from your perspective, considering other perspectives may generate some ideas for your storytelling.

ORIENTED TIMES THREE

Summary

In this chapter you learned about different techniques to keep your audience oriented to your story:
1. Stay oriented to person, place, and time.
2. Decide on a point-of-view (first-person, second-person, third-person) and use it consistently throughout your story.
3. Use the character perspective that lets you tell your story most effectively.

STORY SECRETS FROM SCRIPTURE

7.

PREPARING FOR STORYTIME

In this chapter you will learn about:
- Seven practical techniques to ensure effective delivery of a children's story.

A few gifted storytellers can stand up at any time and deliver a fully-formed, compelling children's story. I do not consider myself to be part of that group. I prefer situations where I have time to plan my story and any supporting materials such as slides, handouts, and props. No one is born speaking in full sentences and delivering structured stories. While it is true that some individuals are blessed to be in families where stories were told early in their lives by verbally-proficient adults, this is not a requirement to develop storytelling skills. We can learn and improve at any point along the journey, but effort and preparation are required.

STORY SECRETS FROM SCRIPTURE

If a children's story is included as part of a program or service, someone believes it to be important. It is vital to ensure the logistical details (audio/visual coordination, preparation of notes), development of the story itself, alignment with other aspects of the service will ensure a maximum impact. Consider these the planning-related texts:

1 CORINTHIANS 14:40 WEB
Let all things be done decently and in order.

PSALM 20:4 NIV
May He give you the desire of your heart and make all your plans succeed.

LUKE 14:28 WEB
Which of you, desiring to build a tower, doesn't first sit down and count the cost, to see if he has enough to complete it?

The Bible also contains narrative accounts related to plans provided by God. God told Noah, "Make yourself an ark … and this is how you shall make it" (Genesis 6:14, 15) and then provided detailed measurements to Noah for the ark. God told Moses, "Let them make Me a sanctuary that I may dwell among them. According to all that I show you … just so you shall make it" (Exodus 25:8, 9).

Developing a story, including introducing and concluding a story, has been covered in previous chapters. Included in this chapter are specific ways to ensure your storytelling experience is the best it can be. These are techniques and tips I have observed in other presenters and applied to my own presentations, whether stories, business presentations or simple communications with others.

Anticipate Audio/Visual Needs

If you are telling stories as part of a regular indoor program, audio/visual support will be necessary. The audio/visual teams at most churches work behind the scenes. If everything runs smoothly, most people don't give them a second thought. However, if the video skips, audio feedback occurs, or an unexpected anomaly happens, you will see heads craned around to see what's happening in the audio/visual booth.

For the children's story, support the audio/visual team by communicating your needs well in advance. Use a microphone, even in a small church. As I tend to use my hands for gesturing during a story, I prefer to use a microphone placed on a stand. This also serves as a great place to tape brief notes. The number of microphones available and the type (wireless or corded) can affect the setup and location for the children's story. Ask the audio/visual team how to turn on and off the microphones. Determining these details in advance will save time and effort when you are ready to tell the children's story.

If you use slides, this needs to be communicated in advance to the audio/visual team. First, get the slides to the audio/visual team either by email, USB thumb drive, airplay, or another way. Second, learn the procedure to advance slides. Will the audio/visual team display and advance the slides? Will you use a remote? If so, know how to operate it. This may seem obvious, but the style and complexity of remotes varies by brand and model.

Keep Notes to a Minimum

It can be tempting to read a written story directly from the source or to write out—word-for-word—your own original story. It is challenging to make reading sound like natural, extemporaneous speech. This is true for sermons as well as stories. It is difficult when reading verbatim to add the inflection, pauses, and emphasis that naturally occurs through talking. Memorizing a story word-for-word has the same effect as reading directly from a script.

Another reason to avoid reading or memorizing a script is that it is easy to get derailed. If you are distracted when reading and lose your place or skip a line, a few seconds may be required to resume the story. The challenge is compounded when using memorized material because you may not be able to find your place again.

Perhaps the best reason for keeping notes to a minimum is to allow more time to engage with your audience, which is primarily children for the purposes of this book. You can make eye contact, adjust the pacing of the story, add more details spontaneously, and enjoy the story experience more yourself. In my business activities I have endured numerous presentations where speakers read slide after slide of paragraphs of text rather than engaging in conversation. While you are the primary speaker as a storyteller, creating an atmosphere to connect with the audience through their nonverbal feedback makes the experience more memorable.

PREPARING FOR STORYTIME

If you have applied the structural model described in this book you already have the basic outline to use for brief notes. Even the written descriptions of the initial situation, complications, etc. may be more than you need to remind yourself of the points of the story.

One of the parables in Chapter 3 is the parable of the unforgiving servant.

If I told this parable as a children's story, my notes would be:
- King forgave servant—massive debt
- Servant to another servant—repay tiny debt
- Servant with small debt thrown into prison
- King to 1st servant: You should have been merciful
- King withdrew forgiveness of massive debt

This is enough detail to keep me on-track. In addition to briefly listing the key points of the story, indicate when to display slides or props, if used.

The easiest way to display these notes is on an index card, in a small notebook or on a notes app on your phone. Hold these in your hand or tape paper notes to a microphone stand. For this story I would use a microphone on a stand to free my hands to demonstrate descriptions like "massive" and "tiny."

Test Out Your Story

Writing out the points of your story to use as notes can take you to a certain level of preparedness and will be helpful as you tell your story. It's possible you may not even need notes to tell your story. Thinking through your story before the actual delivery and telling it to others will build your confidence, reducing the likelihood of awkward pauses. Mental and actual rehearsals help identify gaps and points you might need to clarify. Additionally, the overall flow of telling the story can be enhanced through practice. A rehearsal does not have to be formal with a replication of the setting of your story.

Test out your story with friends and family during conversations and record yourself telling the story. This recording can be audio only or both audio and video. Most of us have phones with apps capable of either style of recording. Listening and 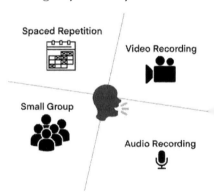 watching yourself is difficult sometimes, but I have always found it to be a helpful exercise. I have always been able to make improvements from watching myself rehearse a story or presentation. This also provides an opportunity to time your story and to adjust if the story is longer or shorter than expected.

Overall, it is helpful to practice telling the story two to three times. Allow time between each telling. This spaced repetition will help with familiarity (even if you use notes).

PREPARING FOR STORYTIME

Be Ready

Contribute to the success of a service or program by being ready to deliver your story at the right time. Unless a service is broadcast live on a network, timing doesn't have to be coordinated to the level of seconds. However, minimizing transition times during a service helps improve the efficiency and provides more time for content, like the sermon, music, and children's story.

Based on the schedule, as the time for the children's story approaches, position yourself near to the designated location. If the children's story occurs on the piano side of the sanctuary, sit on the first or second row. Then, when the children's story is announced, you will be ready to manage any final preparation as children move to the front.

In addition to looking professional and reducing unnecessary waiting time, being positioned in place before the children arrive gives you an opportunity to greet them. It also establishes you, the storyteller, as the authority figure—like a pastor or teacher—during the children's story. Realtors will tell you: location is everything. The same is true during a children's story. Especially if you have props that require space, arriving first will give you an opportunity to mark off the necessary room.

Manage Props for Effectiveness

Not all stories need props, but props bring a tangible element to stories. Even adults like seeing real objects that are relevant to a story or discussion. I recently taught a class on the use of trumpets throughout the Bible. With a few exceptions, most of the trumpets mentioned in the Bible were created from rams' horns, known as shofars. I ordered a shofar from an online retailer and displayed it during the discussion. Several participants came up to look at it and hold it after the discussion. It may not be feasible to bring a physical object to use with every story, but it is impactful when you can.

From the stories I shared in Chapter 5, I would use these objects as props:

Story	Summary	Props	Purpose
Mud on the Carpet	Children knocked over a plant and tried to clean up the spill.	• Small plant • Piece of carpet • Toilet paper • Water • LEGO airplane	Show what knocked over the plant (airplane) and the failed effort at cleaning.
Jim and the Chickens	Jim used a broom to fight with roosters in the chicken coop.	• Broom	Demonstrate fighting with the roosters.
The Abandoned Truck	A group of boys kicked a toy firetruck until it was destroyed.	• Toy firetruck	Simple visual to help children keep focused.
Missionary Goldfish	A missionary bought goldfish for an illustration but did not use them.	• 1-2 goldfish in a small bowl	Simple visual to help children keep focused.

PREPARING FOR STORYTIME

When using props, keep these considerations in mind. First, part of the effectiveness of props is the element of timing. Bring out props only when mentioned in the story but hide them from view when finished. In the story of Jim and the chickens, Jim used the broom but later his sister Lois did not. Putting the broom out of sight fits with the story. In the story about the fire truck, the prop fits with the story after the initial situation. I would say, "And then we saw an abandoned fire truck," and display the prop.

Second, if you are going to use props that start out hidden and then are returned to a hiding place, locate a podium or cloth or something to use as a barrier. This requires planning to setup any props in advance. If the children saw me carrying a firetruck to the front, the element of surprise would be lost.

Third, minimize the use of large props that require time to move into place. This adds preparation time while the audience is waiting and watching. Plus, if children see your props, they may be able to anticipate the story. Ideally, place these props before the children arrive. This provides an opportunity to cover props and creates curiosity.

Fourth, adults and viewers online (if streaming) will be interested in viewing the props. Lift them up for adults and cameras to see them.

Show Slides

If stories include animals, people, and large items beyond the scope of props, using slides is a solution. Like props, slides add extra visual elements to a story. We live in a multimedia age where visuals, whether a prop or an image, are expected. For the parable of the lost sheep it would be logistically challenging to bring in a live sheep for the children's story. I don't even know where I would find a sheep, much less how to get it into the church and keep it hidden until the time for the children's story. An image of a sheep would be satisfactory.

Following the five-part structure, you could have several slides, one for each element of the structure. However, since planning visuals can take time, it is better to decide which specific part of the story would be best served by a visual. In the story of the lost sheep, should it be a bleating sheep who realizes it is lost or a shepherd carrying the sheep? As with props, the slide should only be displayed at the appropriate time. This requires coordination with the audio/visual team.

Since you are using words to tell the children's story, the slides should include images and few words. Research into mental processing has consistently demonstrated that we have two processing pathways into the brain, auditory and visual. Only one input from each pathway can be handled simultaneously. If you have words on the screen and you are speaking different words, listeners don't know what to focus on—their brains can't process two pathways of words. Additionally, research has demonstrated that if you read the words on the screen, audiences tend to stop focusing on both sources of words (storyteller and screen).

PREPARING FOR STORYTIME

Another benefit of using images rather than words on slides is that you don't have to worry about whether the chosen font sizes will be viewable from the back of the room.

These two slides demonstrate the verbal (text) and visual approaches to slide design. In addition to the verbal-verbal conflict discussed above, another significant challenge is that at least a few in your primary audience—children—cannot read. For many reasons, the visual slide is better. It does not conflict with your spoken words, the meaning of the image is immediately grasped, and viewability at a distance is good.

STORY SECRETS FROM SCRIPTURE

Share Handouts

An activity sheet or handout distributed at the end of a story can remind listeners of the story and reinforce learning points. Handouts provide an opportunity to include additional details, links to content shared during the story and activities (crossword puzzles, word searches, etc.) related to the lessons presented in the story. Not every story will benefit from a handout, but they serve a purpose when used judiciously. Using handouts also requires logistical consideration.

Since handouts are printed, allow enough time to design and print the handouts. It is helpful to print more than you might need as you do not want any children to be left out from receiving a handout or having to share with their siblings. Coordinate handouts (if used) with any other handouts that might be used during a service. Occasionally pastors develop an activity sheet for the sermon, often distributed during the children's story.

Another critical factor in the use of handouts is the distribution plan. How will you efficiently and quietly distribute pieces of paper to a large group of excited children? If the next element of a service is dependent on the conclusion of the children's story, time can be lost in managing handout distribution. Ideally, coordinate with a couple of volunteers to help distribute handouts.

PREPARING FOR STORYTIME

Summary

In this chapter you learned about seven practical tips to aid in telling a children's story:
1. Anticipate audio/visual needs.
2. Keep notes to a minimum.
3. Test out your story.
4. Be ready.
5. Manage props for effectiveness.
6. Show slides.
7. Share handouts.

STORY SECRETS FROM SCRIPTURE

8.
AFTER THE STORY

In this chapter you will learn about:
- Packing up after a story.
- Ways to obtain feedback.
- How to plan for more storytelling.

If you picked up this book because you needed some pointers to tell a children's story, hopefully congratulations are in order and your story went well. The Final Situation of your story is not the end of the journey. After you have concluded a story, prepare for the next time you tell a children's story by taking these steps.

Pack-up

While I usually work in my office at home, occasionally I need to work in a nearby cafe. If my wi-fi at home goes out, I know the cafe wi-fi will work as a fast and free backup. Whenever I work from the cafe, I must bring all my items with me: computer, notebook, headphones, phone, and project documentation. The cafe provides a table, power, and wi-fi. When I am ready to leave, I take a moment to verify that the table is as empty as when I arrived and that I have my computer's power supply.

If you used audio/visual support, props, or handouts, take a few minutes to retrieve any media, return the microphone, and gather your props. Additionally, any leftover handouts should be collected. These actions will ensure you do not leave any personal items behind and will ease the burden on the audio/visual and clean-up teams.

Ask for Feedback

When I was in high school, I accompanied a friend on the piano while she sang. I asked my friend Jonathan to turn pages during the performance. With only one page turn remaining, Jonathan accidentally grabbed two pages and turned into the next song. The rest of the performance was a disaster. Afterwards, one of my classmates said, "Doug, that was really bad," something I already knew.

AFTER THE STORY

Unfortunately, this is the type of feedback most listeners provide. In fact, if a storytelling episode missed the mark, most people won't say anything. If it goes well, you will likely hear nonspecific feedback, such as, "That was great!" Or "I enjoyed your story." While these affirmations may cause you to feel good, they do not help improve your storytelling.

A better way to obtain feedback is to simply ask for it. If you have friends or family who heard the story you can ask directly, "For the story I told today, what did you like about?" If they still respond with general comments, you can ask, "What is a detail of the story that you wish I had mentioned?" Receiving specific comments from others is helpful because you can make improvements for the next time you tell a story.

You can also provide your own feedback to yourself if the story was recorded via audio or video. Many churches post services to YouTube or another video streaming platform. Another way to record your storytelling experience is to ask someone to record on a phone while you tell the story. Even if the audio/visual team records a service, having your own recording provides an immediate opportunity to review.

Look to the Future

You've told a story. You've received feedback from others. Now what? It is time to find more opportunities to tell a story and make improvements based on feedback and your own review. If you told the story to friends and family, you can now look for opportunities to share publicly. If you have already told the story as part of a service or program, you can find other places to share the story or storytelling again. Ideally, it would be good to tell the same story two to three times to adjust based on how children reacted, add or remove details to fit the allotted time, and tighten the structure if any part seemed confusing. You may not be able to tell the same story in a different setting right away. The next best solution is to look for new opportunities to tell more stories!

As with feedback, ask to tell a story. Some churches may have a children's story coordinator. Other churches may rely on the speaker or worship coordinator to find participants for a service or program. While this book has been focused on telling children's stories are part of a worship service, these same techniques work for any setting: vacation Bible school, children's Bible study classes, and wherever storytelling occurs. Consider these settings as well when looking for ways to share stories through storytelling.

Final Situation

We have reached the Final Situation of this book. In the middle chapters you read about the five-part structure with examples from Jesus' parables, saw how Jesus approached parables, learned about ways to find stories, and discovered how to enhance the storytelling experience by using slides, props, handouts, and audio/visual support effectively. You now know the *Story Secrets from Scripture* and you are ready to develop and deliver children's stories for worship, VBS, and Bible study.

AFTER THE STORY

Summary

In this chapter you learned about actions to take after telling a story:
1. Gather any props and media.
2. Identify ways to improve your story and storytelling by asking others for feedback and reviewing any recordings.
3. Look for additional opportunities to share by telling stories in the same setting and looking for a different setting.

STORY SECRETS FROM SCRIPTURE

–A–
Abundance
Acceptance
Advent
Altar
Anointed
Ask
Atonement
Authority

–B–
Baptism
Beginning
Believe
Birth
Blameless
Blessing
Books
Bread
Bride

–C–
Called
Celebration
Character
Charity
Children
Chosen
Church
Cleanse
Clothing
Coming
Commandments
Commitment
Communion
Community
Compassion
Confess
Converted
Covenant
Creation
Creator
Crown

–D–
Death
Deliverance
Disciple
Dominion

–E–
Encouragement
End
Endurance
Eternity

–F–
Faith
Faithfulness
Fasting
Father
Fellowship
Firstfruits
Follow
Forever
Forgiveness
Found
Free
Freedom
Friendship
Fruit
Fulfillment

–G–
Generosity
Gentleness
Gift
Giving
Glory
God
Goodness
Gospel
Grace
Growth

–H–
Harvest
Healing
Heart
Heaven
Heritage
Holiness
Holy Spirit
Home
Honor
Hope
Hospitality
Humanity
Humility
Hypocrisy

–I–
Identity
Image
Inheritance
Innocent
Instruction

–J–
Journey
Joy
Jubilee
Justice
Justify

–K–
Kindness
King
Kingdom
Knowledge

–L–
Law
Learning
Life
Light

THEMES IN THE BIBLE

Living
Longsuffering
Lost
Love

—M—
Marriage
Martyr
Meditate
Memorial
Mercy
Message
Messenger
Messiah
Ministry
Mission
Morality
Mystery

—N—
Need
Neighbor

—O—
Obedience
Offering
Oneness
Overcoming

—P—
Patience
Peace
Perfection
Perseverance
Pity
Power
Praise
Prayer
Preparation
Pride
Priest
Promise

Prophecy
Prophet
Provide
Purity

—R—
Reconstruction
Redeemed
Refuge
Reign
Rejoice
Remission
Remnant
Repentance
Representative
Respect
Rest
Restoration
Resurrection
Return
Revelation
Reverence
Reward
Righteousness

—S—
Sabbath
Sacred
Sacrifice
Salvation
Sanctify
Sanctuary
Sealed
Seek
Self-control
Selfishness
Servant
Serve
Share
Shepherd
Signs

Sin
Slavery
Son
Soul
Sovereignty
Spirit
Strength
Submission
Suffering
Symbol

—T—
Teaching
Tenderness
Testimony
Testing
Thanksgiving
Throne
Tithe
Transgression
Treasure
Tribulation
Trinity
Trust
Truth

—U—
Understanding
Unity

—V—
Victory
Virgin

—W—
Washed
Will
Wisdom
Witness
Word
Worship
Worthy

About the Author

Douglas G. Pratt is a life-long learner who resides with his wife and daughter near Chattanooga, Tennessee. Born to teachers (Mom-English, Dad-Computer Technology), Doug writes frequently about more effective ways to communicate and learn. He graduated from Southern Adventist University with a degree in behavioral science and from Middle Tennessee State University with a master's degree in clinical psychology. Doug shares pictures and infographics on Instagram and contributes to NotesForLearning.com, a blog with posts covering technology, communication, note taking and learning.

Made in the USA
Columbia, SC
26 November 2024